BLOGGING
BRILLIANTLY
For Your Business

BLOGGING
BRILLIANTLY
For Your Business

30 DAYS TO DOMINATE YOUR MARKET

Christine Tremoulet

Vivid & Brave Media

HOUSTON, TEXAS

Vivid & Brave Media
PO Box 7048
Houston, Texas 77248

www.VividAndBrave.com

Ordering Information:

Quantity sales. Special discounts are available on quantity purchases by corporations, associations, and others. For details, contact the publisher at the address above.

Printed in the United States of America
First Printing, 2016
ISBN 978-0692654354

For more information about Christine Tremoulet, visit her website at www.ChristineTremoulet.com

Being bold is not about being loud;
it is about being VULNERABLE
and bringing your story into the light.

— CHRISTINE TREMOULET

CONTENTS

Getting Started

Throughout this book, I am sharing the secrets and strategies I've learned over 16+ years as a successful blogger and business owner. These are time tested, and ready for you to implement.

I was a business owner before I was a blogger, but only by a year or so. In the late 1990s, I started a business making soap and selling it online. In the fall of 2000, when I had hung up my soapmaker apron and taken a job as a web consultant for a design agency in Houston, working with Fortune 500 companies on their web presence strategy, I started my first blog. I had no idea what a pivotal moment in my life that would be; everything about my life today I can trace back to that first blog.

In the early years of blogging, we did not focus on any one single niche, and no one was doing it for their business. At least not directly. Blogs were a place where you shared whatever you were thinking at the moment, much like many of us use Facebook today. One post might be a profound post on current events, and the next post might be about what you ate for lunch that day.

In 2002, I started a hosting company that focused on hosting websites for bloggers while still working as a web consultant. It was during that time that I first met Matt Mullenweg, and he told me that he was working on a new blogging software. I mentioned to him that I was great at naming things, a skill developed during my soapmaking days, and to let me know if he needed help. In 2003, while we were at SXSW Interactive, he told me he was ready to launch the beta version, but he needed a name. Days later, I called him and left a voicemail with my suggestion. That is how I ended up naming WordPress.

Somewhere in this time, a few businesses started using blogs to promote themselves. It was a great way to stand out in a crowded market then, as it still is today. It would still be a few years before it caught on.

In 2006, I sold my hosting company. I was one of the success stories of the early dotcom era. Now I needed

Since I was a teenager, I dreamed of being a professional photographer. It always seemed an impossible dream; I had convinced myself that the only options were to work for a newspaper or National Geographic. (Which is still on my dream job list.) Thanks to blogging, and sharing my photographs online, I was gaining recognition among my readers as being a photographer, and I realized that there were many other options I could explore.

In 2007, I first opened the doors on my photography business online. Initially testing the waters with a variety of photography sessions, by the summer I had determined that wedding photography was my favorite, and I launched a new website and blog focused on that. I linked to my personal blog so people could find that as well.

I was fully booked my first full year in business with minimal effort. Over and over again, when I would have my initial meeting with potential clients, they would tell me that I sounded exactly the same in person as I did online.

I always knew that blogs were powerful; it was then that I realized that they are critical to business success online.

It wasn't just my business blog that people were reading; they were spending time reading the archives of my personal blog as well, and following me on social media. They wanted to know more about ME, not just about my business.

The Houston photography industry is heavily saturated to begin with, and there were more photographers starting their business every day. I stood out in the crowd because of how accessible I was to potential clients. They were able to learn about me, what I stood for, and why they should want me there for their wedding day. We connected on a personal level.

The success of my business was due to sharing who I am, not just what I do.

In a sea of choices, when all other factors were equal – the quality of photographs, the price, the options available, where everyone is truly doing the same thing – I stood out to them because of what I shared online.

Blogging takes time and work, but it has always been the best investment in my business that I could make.

I ran a successful photography business for 8 years; during that time, I looked back at all of my business experience and realized that my favorite part of being a business owner is the community of entrepreneurs. As much as I love photography, I love even more helping others grow their businesses online.

In 2015, I made the decision to focus full time on helping other entrepreneurs, especially photographers. This book is only the start; it is the foundational basis of steps that I took over the span of 30 days to improve my own blog. As I did the work, I was inspired to share the steps with others so that they could do the work too.

The core of my philosophy can be summed up as this: others can do what you do. They can copy what you sell. They can try to emulate your style. They can compete on price. They can never BE you. This is why your online presence should not focus around what you do, but who you are. Unique and beautifully different.

It is my sincere wish for you that blogging brilliantly will change the course of your business, and bring you the same success that it has always brought to me.

Blogging for Business vs the Business of Blogging

One thing I should make clear is that the focus is on how to blog for your business. Not making a business out of a blog. In writing, the two things sound very similar, but in fact they are quite different. While some of these tips may help you if your goal is to be a professional blogger, the focus is helping your blog be the cornerstone of your online marketing efforts to grow your business.

The business of blogging often focuses on being sponsored by companies for promoting products, making money off of advertising on your website, and sometimes selling products of their own.

These tips were developed with people that market products or services through their website, directly to their ideal customers.

How This Book is Set Up

The book is divided in to steps you can take over the next 30 days; do one chapter a day, and your blog will be far ahead of where it is right now. It is ok if you can't work at that pace; do the tasks when you can. Each chapter ends with homework that can do immediately to improve your blog.

In addition to this book, please join us in our Facebook community for additional conversation about business, marketing online, branding, blogging and more at http://Facebook.com/Groups/ BusinessBrilliantly

What is Measured Grows

As you start to work your way through this book, I recommend creating a chart with your current blog and social media stats. This will allow you to see your progress over the next 30 days, and the months ahead.

My chart has the name of each blog and social media account across the top, and the weeks listed down the side.

Every week, I record the number of visitors to my blog in the previous week, the number of fans I have on my Facebook Page, and the number of followers I have on Twitter, Instagram, and Pinterest. What you choose to track is up to you – you may have more items, or less.

Having a measure of where you started will help you to see the impact that the changes you are making is having on your business. Even if the growth is small, if you follow all of the steps in this book? It will happen.

Just Getting Started with Blogging?

This course was built around helping you refresh your blog, kick start it, and use it to dominate your market. I realize though that you may not have a blog at all. That is ok, there are still plenty of tips ahead that you can use to help your business online! While I won't be covering specifics on how to set up your blog, there are many sites that do a great job of covering that information.

WordPress.org or WordPress.com?

WordPress.org is the self-hosted version of WordPress and the one that I recommend. It allows for the most flexibility, and it is free for commercial and personal use. It does require monthly hosting and purchasing a domain, which will have costs associated to it..

WordPress.com on the other hand is free as well, but not for commercial use. If you have a business, or you ever want to run ads on your site, you will have to pay to use WordPress.com. You are also limited on only using the themes and plugins offered.

The key factors that you want from a host is reliability, speed (if your site loads slowly it will impact your readers and your SEO), and quality customer support. Read reviews online of the different companies before you select one.

Tutorials for Setting up WordPress

There are many great tutorials online with information on how to set up WordPress. Depending on the hosting company you select, they may offer tutorials specific to their service. Here are others that you can review.
Michael Hyatt's EZ WordPress Setup:

http://michaelhyatt.com/ez-wordpress-setup.html
BlogTyrant's WordPress Blog Instructions:
http://www.blogtyrant.com/wordpress-blog/
Molly Greene's How to Set Up a Free WordPress Blog:
http://www.molly-greene.com/how-to-set-up-a-free-wordpress-blog/

Please note: while Michael Hyatt & BlogTyrant both mention Bluehost in their tutorials, you can do the same steps with most other hosting companies.

Should You Consider Squarespace?

Squarespace is also a great option if you want someone to handle things for you when you are building your website. Hosting, updates, everything you need for setting up and designing your website is included. Similar to WordPress.com, they will host the website for you.

There are many beautiful design templates to choose from. They do not have plugins, but the Squarespace team keeps an eye on the most popular WordPress plugins and add the similar functions to their service.

I recommend SquareSpace to people who do not mind less flexibility or the lack of plugins, and who want the service options that it includes.

CHAPTER ONE

Why You Need A Blog For Your Business

Whenever I tell someone I have blogged for 16 years, I am often asked the same question: "Do you think blogs are still important?" Have you ever wondered that?

I'm here to tell you ... YES. Yes. Yes. OMG YES. Very much, yes.

You still need a blog for your business. The biggest reason? Your website is your storefront online. Your blog is where your customers come to interact with you. Just you, no flashing & blinking ads and private messages to distract them like over on social media. When it comes to your blog, it is just the two of you.

You have a HUGE opportunity here to connect with people through your blog, but only if you choose to take it.

Let's think back to how it used to be. Before people were online. Before any of us had heard of the Internet, blogging, or social media. Back then, if you had a business it was in some physical location. People came in to your store and interacted with you.

Imagine you are in some idyllic setting in the 1950s, and you have just left the hair salon or the barber shop where you had your hair done and gossiped with the other customers about what is happening in town. Now you head in to the shop next door, and you see the owner at the cash register.

You greet her with a friendly hello, and she says nothing personal back, no greeting, no conversation. She simply responds by just by pointing out products. "Here is a pair of shoes. They come in 9 different sizes. You can buy them in 4 different colors. Would you like a pair of shoes?"

You are puzzled, but you continue to try to talk with her. Instead of responding, she adds in a rather dull monotone voice, "Here is a purse. It matches the shoes. It comes in 4 colors, plus black, white, and brown."

Meanwhile, you are want to have a conversation. "Susan, how is your day going?" She says nothing in response. "Oh, did you hear the latest news?" You keep trying, telling her about the gossip you just heard at the salon.

Crickets and a blank stare. No connection at all.

At this point in time, you would probably wonder what on earth was going on. Out of frustration, you would leave. You would go off to another store, where the owner did not like she was animatronic. You'd have a conversation, you would chat, you would connect, you would share stories with the owner of the next store you visited.

You would buy from the person you connected with, even if their products were more expensive, because people buy from people that they like.

Which Store Do You Want Yours to Be?

Your website is just like the first store if you're not interacting with your potential clients and customers through your blog.

How most people treat their website today is not how stores worked 60 years ago. Realizing that and incorporating who you are and what you are passionate about? That makes all the difference for your site readers and future clients.

Your 1950s shopping experience would have included being ushered in as a friend, and a valued guest. There would be conversation, whether it was light chatting or something much more deep.

You would feel as though you were KNOWN and UNDERSTOOD.

You're not a robot. You are unique, and you bring to your business something that no one else can: your personality. Your stories, the topics you are passionate about, the very things that drive you to have built the business you have created? No one else has those things in exactly the same way that you do.

Sharing yourself with the world through your blog? That is the key to dominating your market.

It is what will attract people to you, because they will have a sense that they know you.

Don't be the robot just showing off your products and services. Anyone can do that. Share about them and show the world you are full of life.

The Power Of The Internet Has Shifted

15 years ago, the power of the Internet was that it could make even a small company look large. Now, thanks to blogs and other social media outlets, the tables have turned. We DEMAND that every company acts as if they are small. We want to connect with them on a personal level.

Use that to your advantage.

Your blog is the center of your social media universe. All of your social media should reflect back to your blog.

Social media platforms lead people to your blog, and your blog leads them to hire you.

Facebook, Twitter, Instagram, Pinterest – all of them feed in to our need for instant gratification. They feel quick and easy, and all it takes is for someone to click "Like" or a heart to let you know that they like what you have to say.

The problem with social media is that it has such a short shelf life. It is rare if someone will go back through more than a week of your social media posts. With blog posts? If a potential client is interested in working with you, they will go through your archives on your blog for as long as they have time. They will dig in and get to know you. They more they do this, the more they connect with you and like you. It will dramatically increase your chances of booking them as a client.

No matter how active you are on other accounts, your blog is always the Sun in your solar system, with the other accounts rotating around it. It needs to be at the core of your focus. You want to use your presence on other social media accounts to bring people back to your blog, so they can learn from there how to work with you.

HOMEWORK

Look through your blog posts and find one where you did not show much personality at all. Maybe you held back because you thought you had to be super professional to be taken seriously?

What edits can you make to that post to spice it up, to make it sound like you are talking to a friend? Edit it so that your readers can connect with you and THEN...

Share that new, fresh, PERSONABLE post on social media. Your choice as to where. (Please come share it in our Facebook group as well when you introduce your-self!)

CHAPTER TWO

The Most Common Fears About Blogging

When the topic of blogging comes up, there are fears that are closely linked to it for most people. Today we will work on overcoming the moments of doubt that might block you from sharing your brilliance online.

- What if no one reads my site?
- What if someone (often a family member is mentioned) reads my site?
- What if I run out of things to talk about?
- What if I don't have enough time?
- What if someone realizes I have a business?

What if No One Reads My Site?

You're right - if you're just starting out? No one might read your site at first. Even if you've been doing this for several years, only a small handful of people might be reading your site.

When you see people talk about having 10,000 visitors a day to their website, it feels insurmountable. Big. Enormous. Pressure.

You can define your own success.

Step back, and take a deep breath. Now think about it for a moment what does success look like FOR YOU?

What are your goals for your business? For your life?

You are allowed to define what success looks like for you. Your success might be 50 visitors a day. Maybe you only take on 4 new clients a month, and having 50 visitors highly engaged visitors a day is plenty to meet your marketing goals.

Possibly you really do want 10,000 visitors a day. You have a product of some form to sell that hundreds of people can buy at the same time, you have no limits there, so you want all the eyes on your site that you can get.

Do you know where those sites with 10,000 readers a day started? With 1 reader a day.

Everyone starts at the same place. Do not compare where you are right now with someone else's highlight reel.

If you never start, if you never put yourself out there, if you never tell the world that you are an expert? No one will ever know. People care about what you have to say. They want you to share what you know with them.

We all have days where we struggle with feeling inadequate. Your business? It goes on without you, whether you feel like you are good enough or not. It needs you to help it thrive. You are at the very core of it, and you are the spark that will ignite the success of it. You just have to show up.

What if Someone Reads My Site?

In order to grow engagement on your blog, I'm going to encourage you to be vulnerable. To share your stories, because they are what make you unique from anyone else in your market. They are what make you stand out from your competition.

It is up to you to set the line of what is too vulnerable that you do not want to cross. For some people, they prefer to keep things very light and on the surface level, especially on their business site. For other people, they pour their passions on the table and share it all. Where you fall in this is up to you.

If you are concerned about someone reading something? Don't post it online. Anywhere. Not on your blog, but also not in your email, on Facebook, or Twitter. (Even in a private groups or conversations.)

You can delete things online, but screenshots seem to always make their way back where they don't belong. So if you do not want them to read it? Do not post it.

I am a pretty open book and over the past 16 years as a blogger, I have written a lot of very personal things online. I use what I call the "Mom Test": if my mom was to read the post, am I going to get a phone call about it? If

I was to call me about it, do I want to have that conversation? Do I believe in what I wrote to the point that I would stand up for it? Or is it not worth the fight? If my convictions are strong, I'll still post it. (Maybe not on my business blog, but this same rule applies to Facebook and anywhere else online.)

What if I Run Out of Things to Talk About?

We are going to work together though this to make sure you have plenty to write about. If you love what you do? Coming up with 1 post per week should not be hard. I'll be sharing tips on things that I do to help me come up with content when I'm stuck, ways to overcome writer's block, all of that. If you commit to the process, I'm confident you will have 52 ideas at least by the end of this.

I have to be honest though and say that this has happened to me in the past. I thought I wanted to blog about a topic so I set up a new website. I did not have a plan, and I had not brainstormed blog post ideas before I launched it. I wrote a handful of posts, and then I just stopped. I was stuck. No words were coming out. I dreaded it every time I thought about writing a post there.

It took time and me stepping back to look at what was happening to figure it out. As passionate as I am about the topic of that blog? I could hold a conversation about it for a few hours at most.

On the other hand, ask me to talk about blogging, marketing, branding, pricing, social media - anything related to getting your business in front of your clients? I can go on for days. Maybe even months. My list of blog post ideas for these topics? It seems to be never ending.

It was simply a matter of getting clear on what I was most passionate about talking about for my business.

Once I got back on track? I used the same tips I'll be sharing with you, and I doubt I'll run out of things to write about any time soon.

If you want to talk about a topic, but you do not have a lot to say on it, instead of starting a new website, consider adding it to your main blog as a small series of posts. Maybe once a month, or once a week? That way, you can share your thoughts on it without committing to writing about it on a regular basis.

Your clients will love this opportunity to get to know another side of you that they might not know about otherwise. You will become multi-dimensional for them online.

What if I don't Have Enough Time?

Oh, time. Always in limited supply, for everyone. First and foremost? You are going to want to make time for this, because blogging will help you bring in more clients. It will help your business grow. It will help you stay connected to the clients you already have, and to people who are interested in your business and considering hiring you.

If you ran that store on Main Street, would you ever say you didn't have time to go open the front doors to let your customers in?

There are many options here, some are free and some are not:

- Write a little every day; your posts do not have to be long; focus on preparing one a week. It is suggested that long posts do better in SEO, but that doesn't matter much if you're not writing anything at all. Some is better than none.

- Plan out your posts so that you can write several at one time if that works with your writing style.

- Create a system for blogging so that the process is streamlined for you.

- Dictate your posts while you do other things. For example, Dragon NaturallySpeaking would transcribe your posts for you as you talk. You'll just need to review it and clean up any errors.

- Use a voice recorder app on your phone or computer and then hire someone to transcribe it for you.

- Hire a copywriter to help you with your site. You are going to want to be careful with this one and make sure that they can write close to how you speak. If there is a disconnect between the two, people might pick up on this when they inquire about working with you.

- A Virtual Assistant could help with creating graphics, scheduling social media posts, and a number of other items.

What if Someone Realizes I Have a Business?

I was being a little cheeky when I added this one, but then I realized it actually happens quite often. I see many websites that don't have a call to action, a way to buy a product, no store, no option to work with the owner ... nothing.

It is as if people are afraid to tell the world that they have a business.

I'm not saying that that is you, but just in case - go check your website. Are you telling people that you have a business? That they can come and buy things from you? Or are you hiding it away and hoping that they figure it out?

You've got this.

You can do it. I promise. It is time to set the fears aside, and move beyond the blocks. That is the only way to go forward.

HOMEWORK

Share what you do, in some way, shape, or form on social media. Take one action today to be visible and overcome your fear of vulnerability. It can be a link to your site, a product or a post on social media. Consider writing a fresh blog post. Get in front of the people that are looking for you. If you share on social media, be sure to use the #BusinessBrilliantly hashtag so that we can cheer you on.

CHAPTER THREE

Embrace The Power Of Your Personal Brand

It is time to embrace your already existing personal brand.

Yes, you have a personal brand, even if you have never thought about it before. You are a walking, talking, living, breathing personal brand.

Since you are at the very heart of your company, it is time to embrace it. Even if you are not comfortable with the concept of a personal brand.

Head Marketer for Brand YOU

"Regardless of age, regardless of position, regardless of the business we happen to be in, all of us need to understand the importance of branding. We are CEOs of our own companies: Me Inc. To be in business today, our most important job is to be head marketer for the brand called

You." – Tom Peters, Fast Company Magazine ("A Brand Called You"
http://www.fastcompany.com/28905/brand-called-you)

Even though this article came out originally in print back in 1997, you should read it. It is FASCINATING.

Your personal brand is not just who you are, it is what other people think of when they think of you. Your control over it is limited by what you put out there, but your personal brand is also impacted by what other people reflect back and say to you – or about you when you are not around.

This impacts you, whether you are an entrepreneur or working for someone else. It doesn't matter, you have a personal brand.

Your Personal Brand – Online

We are much wiser than we were back in 1997 when that article I linked above first came out. We have learned that anything that we put out there online will stick with us forever. (I mean, I hope you have learned that. You do realize that, right?)

Some people would say that you can then curate your life. I agree, in part – after all, if you stage your house for your Pinterest photo shoot and it normally is a hot mess, you're probably going to hide that hot mess part from me. Society has always had things that are considered taboo, things that you just don't talk about. Ideas have shifted dramatically in the past 40 years, and things once taboo are normal to us now; we have just replaced them with new taboos in our Perfection Culture.

The important lesson here is to bring the personal back in to your brand.

As a service-based entrepreneur, WHO you are matters more than your products because your clients are choosing you. They want to know who they are working with. They want to know what you love, and why you love it. Not just in your work, but in your life.

The more touchpoints that you give them to connect, the deeper that connection can be.

By living, you already are a Personal Brand.

Show it off. Tell the world. Give them a reason to love you, allow them to know you. Tell them your story. Not just the big grand moments, but the small daily ones.

As humans, we connect the most deeply over our non-critical flaws. Our quirks. Our passions.

If you're trying to be all business all the time, it does not benefit you. If a client has three options, with reviews, price, and quality of work all the same? The thing that will impact their decision the most is the personal connection. Who do they like? That person will win the job. They will even find a way to pay MORE for them if they can.

Creating a Visual Representation of Your Personal Brand

As you design your website and blog, having a clear visual representation of your personal brand is essential.

When I work with my coaching clients, I encourage them to create a mood board of elements that they love so that they can clearly see the trends & styles that they are most drawn to.

In order to do this, you need to gather photographs of things that you love. These photos can come from anywhere. You can gather them from magazines. You can pin photographs on Pinterest. You can go through a store or your local mall and take photographs with your phone.

Look for logos that you love. Packaging that appeals to you. Colors that stand out for you. Look at things that are nothing like the products that you sell; I have used photographs of outfits that I like, the yarn that I own, my favorite blanket. Anything that you find attractive? Save a photograph of it.

Once you have a large collection of images, look at the images. What trends do you see? Are there designs that keep coming up repeatedly? Colors that you have selected over and over? Fonts that are in use? Are they minimalist images? Bold & vibrant? Full of texture? What stands out to you?

Keeping these images in mind as you design a website, or providing them to a web designer if you choose to hire one, will help you develop a consistent and recognizable brand for your business, one that is authentic to you and what you love.

Are You Giving Your Potential Clients the Chance to Like YOU?

Your personal brand already exists. Are you tapping in to it? Making the most of it? I can find so much out about you online if I want to as it is; are you taking advantage of that power and using it to make yourself stand out in your market?

Even when you feel that you have nothing unique to say, that you are not that exciting, remember that no one else has the combination of everything that you do. Your future clients are looking for you and they want to know that you are the right one for them.

HOMEWORK

Think about what makes up YOUR personal brand, and then create a story, image or even just a quote that embodies it. Share about it on your blog or social media. Gather photographs to create a brand inspiration board so that your blog & social media graphics have a strong, cohesive feel in the future.

CHAPTER FOUR

Goals? We've Got SMART Ones!

It is so easy to get wrapped up in the day-to-day of running your business and your blog. But what are you working towards? What is the plan?

Having goals for your blog isn't exactly working on your blog, but it is working FOR your blog.

SMART goals for your blog & your business make it easy to decide what to do next!

Setting goals that are SMART has had a major impact on my business. I'm normally an "I've got an idea, I am going to test it out, and if it works – YAY!" sort of person. 10 year plans? Oh goodness, no. 5 year plans? Who knows what I'll be doing in 5 years!

1 year plans? Or even better, 6 month plans? I can totally get behind those! Having set them this year has helped me be much more focused. Turns out I needed some SMART goals.

(To those of you that can do 5 and 10 year plans, I bow in respect. Seriously. I wish I could do that!)

Are You Setting Goals that are SMART?

In order to make sure that you are making SMART goals, you need to make sure that they are covering all of these aspects:

Specific– target a specific area for improvement. You can't be vague here! You need to know exactly what you're working towards. Use the 5 W's to help you determine this – Who, What, Where, When & Why.

Measurable– quantify or at least suggest an indicator of progress. You need a way to measure or to keep score. Numbers matter here.

Attainable– I am all for big dreams, but when it comes to setting goals? Break it down in to bite-size pieces that you can reach.

Realistic– state what results can realistically be achieved, given available resources.

Time-related– give yourself a deadline to review and readjust.

You decide that you will get more business. Awesome … but is that a SMART goal?

No – it is way too vague! How will you do it? What does "more business" look like? When will you achieve it by? What is the definition of "more business"? When will you know if you've hit it?

What if you said that over the next 6 months you will double the number of visitors to your blog? Now you have a specific area to focus on, something to measure, it is attainable (with some work), it is realistic (unless you have 1 million visitors a day already), and you have set a time frame for it.

Before you start, you will want to look at what has worked for you in the past. If you tried something already and it had amazing results, how can you continue that? You need to know where you are starting from in order to decide where you are going.

Don't be afraid to take chances though – if you have an idea that you think might just work? Go for it!

Goals to Consider for Your Blog

- How many readers will your blog gain in the next 6 months? How much will your traffic increase?
- How much income will you bring in over the next six months / year?
- What series of blog posts could you start to bring readers back to your blog?
- How many blog posts will you write a week?
- How much will you interact on Social Media?
- How much will you grow your Social Media following on Twitter, Facebook, Instagram & Pinterest?
- How many new clients will you bring in per week/month/year (depending on how your business works)?

•   Is your site due for a design overhaul? When will you have it done by?

•   Is it time to update your static pages on your website? (About, Pricing, Work with Me, Media Kit, etc.)

•   Does your business need systems in place to make things run more smoothly? What do you need to do to set those up?

•   You'll go through the Blogging Brilliantly series by a certain date?

Once you decide on your SMART goals, you can start to set up tasks to do to get you there, and before you know it you'll be zooming right along to achieving them!

HOMEWORK

Set your goals & decide how you want to track them. Make sure that they are SMART so that you can celebrate when you reach them!

CHAPTER FIVE

Get Analytical – Add Google Analytics to Your Blog

We're about to dive in to creating an editorial calendar so you know what content to write and you can plan around your marketing schedule, but there is really no point in starting up any of that if you're not taking the time to analyze what is already happening on your blog.

First things first? You need to add Google Analytics to your blog if you do not have it already. Then you can plan your editorial calendar and what content you will write to attract your clients.

Go now to Analytics and sign up for an account. (http://www.google.com/analytics/) Google will then provide you with a snippet of code to add to your website pages. If you follow their instructions for setting up Analytics they mention pasting the code in to every page you want to track.

You most likely don't have to do this though! YAY! Most WordPress themes have an area where you add the Analytics code for the theme – often in the design options.

This part will vary from theme to theme, so I can't really help you here by telling you where to go. Poke around and see what you find. This is one of the best parts of using WordPress for a website – the theme is the design framework for your content, and so you only have to enter it one time.

If your theme doesn't have a specific place to add this, you can find a number of WordPress Plugins that will make it easy for you. My first choice would be Google Analytics by Yoast:

https://yoast.com/wordpress/plugins/google-analytics/)

Now that you have Analytics in place, we can start looking at some ways to use it to help you plan things for the future on your blog!

PS - A lesson I learned the hard way: be sure to double check from time to time and make sure you have it in place. I changed WordPress themes, and in the process I forgot to add the code to the new theme. I didn't know for a few weeks, so nothing was tracked in the meantime!

HOMEWORK

This is an easy one - get analytics on your blog! Then start watching to see what your readers are visiting the most.

CHAPTER SIX

I Think I Recognize You?
Brand YOU!

If you walked in to a coffee shop to meet a new client, would they recognize you? Would they connect the person walking in the door with the one they had seen on your website?

If I passed you in the hall at a conference after talking to you online for the past 6 months, would I know who you are? If I followed your blog and then connected with you on Twitter, Facebook, Pinterest, Instagram – would I see you there?

You need to have a photograph of you on your website. It is how your clients and your site visitors will connect with you emotionally. Putting a name to the face.

More importantly, that photo needs to look like YOU. Today. Not you 10 years ago. Not you on your wedding day. Not you with a camera blocking most of your face. Or a book. Or a computer. (Your clients already know what you do, that is why they are at your website. You don't need to prove it to them by holding up something in front of you.) Not your kids, your dog, or your favorite flower.

YOU. Right now. As you are.

Brand YOU with the same photograph on your blog and all of your social media accounts. Be recognizable!

Having the same avatar photo across all of your social media properties helps people on a subconscious level connect with you. Over and over, they are seeing your face. It is building brand recognition, and connection. Isn't that what we all want, after all?

Your Photo Represents Your Brand.

Let's take my photo for example. My clothing choice for my avatar photo and the lipstick I am wearing is very intentional for the message I want to convey. I'm wearing a black & white striped shirt, a floral scarf, and bold lipstick. I wear stripes regularly; I'm pretty sure every shirt I own is either stripes, or black because I like the contrast with my hair, but I pair it with a bold scarf or necklace almost all the time.

What can you guess about my branding just from seeing that? I am vivacious and adventurous. I love nature. I am bold. A little loud. I stand out in the crowd. I'm perfectly ok with the fact that I have gray hair, or as I call it "sexy silver".

These things are also all core values of my brand – I want you to be authentic, see your beauty, and be confident about it. I want you to be a little daring and push your limits, exploring what just might happen if you step out of bounds. If my photo had been edited to be very soft, if I was wearing more muted clothing and I had on a more neutral lipstick, and if I wasn't looking so directly at the camera – it would completely change the feeling that you have when you see my photograph.

I am my brand. A walking embodiment of it, and it all starts when you connect with that photograph.

I know it is hard because you like to change your Facebook avatar weekly, but every time you do that? I have to look twice when I see your posts there. I'm missing the visual cue that quickly tells me it is you.

Psychologists have even studied how this impacts people. If you use a different image on all of your web properties, that is what you're doing to your clients. Each time, they have to ask themselves, "Is that the same person"?

Help them make the connection more easily. Represent yourself with the same photograph everywhere.

HOMEWORK

Brand YOU! Find a current photo that you love of yourself, or have a new one taken. Yes, it is time to get in front of the camera and have someone else take a new photo of you if you need it.

Your BIG GOAL is to make sure it is recognizable, and represents your brand well. Think about the colors you are wearing and if they coordinate with your branding. Think about how you want the photograph to feel – are you lighthearted and fun? Vivacious? Elegant & timeless? Cosmopolitan?

Whatever fits YOU and what you want your brand to evoke, go for that feeling in the photograph.

Once you have your new picture, go post it everywhere. Add it to your About page. Make it your Gravatar for when you post comments online, put it on Facebook, use it on Instagram, Pinterest, Twitter, LinkedIn, wherever you are online. Change it on Skype. Any place you can put a photo, change it out. Brand yourself.

Bonus Tip: add your photograph somehow on your business card if you can. Later on, it will be quick & easy for people to remember who you are if they see your face there. People tend to remember faces before they remember names! (I have a personal theory that they are less likely to throw away a card with your photo on it as well!)

CHAPTER SEVEN

Introduce Yourself

While some people opt for a very minimalist blog layout, streamlined with one column of text and images, many of us have a blog that has a sidebar off on one side.

Take advantage of that sidebar real estate on your blog!

It doesn't have to be long and drawn out – matter of fact, it is best if you link to your About page for all of the in depth details about yourself. Make sure it is at the very top, before anything else. You are more important than the links to your social media accounts or your email list.

Here are the things you want to be sure to include:

•   The lovely photograph of yourself that you took recently, the one that you've added to all of your social media accounts as well.

•   Your name, because people connect with people over all else. They want to know who you are!

- Tell your readers why they are here, in one sentence. What is the purpose of your website?
- Make sure they know where you are located and how to contact you. Even if you work with clients around the world, they like to know where you are located.
- If you want to include a sentence or two to help them get to know you even better, share your why, your hobbies, the names of your pets, whatever the case may be – this is a great spot for it. Keep it short.
- At the end, you can add a link to your longer About page.
- Below THAT, you can include links to your social media profiles – just the active ones, please!

We will talk more about the About Me page soon. For now, these quick changes will help people connect with you, which is the whole mission of your blog.

I can already hear some of you saying how you're boring, and your clients don't want to know you – you just want to show off your work and be done with it. Or that you're a terrible writer.

Those voices? Well, I don't agree with any of them.

We've talked already about your website being your virtual storefront. If I walked in to your storefront and you didn't even smile at me, and then you used a monotone voice to just tell me what you're selling and who you've sold things to in the past, and then you walked away without any interaction with me, do you think I'd have any interest in shopping at your store?

HELLLLLLLLLL NO. I'd go down the block to find the next store (because on the internet, there is always a next store) and then they would greet me with a smile and a cup of cool ice tea, while asking me how my day was, sharing a personal story about themselves, maybe one about how they made something and what was the passion that fueled the creation? Oh goodness. I am ALL IN.

That is the power of blogging, my friends. Introduce yourself. Share your stories, the passion that drives you, the reason you're a creative entrepreneur.

You have the power to change the world. It is time to be vulnerable.

PS – Your social media accounts also have places for you to introduce yourself. Make sure that they are up to date with your current details!

HOMEWORK

Check out your sidebar on your site and your social media accounts. Do they scream YOU, or do they mumble?

Another great option is to add an Author Box to your posts. I use the Starbox plugin on my WordPress site, but there are many out there that you can choose from.

CHAPTER EIGHT

Are You Making It Hard For People To Contact You?

Yay! You have people visiting your blog! Mission accomplished!

Except … now they can't figure out where you're located at or how to contact you. So they leave and go find someone else. Not exactly your goal, is it?

Look at your blog as if you're a first time visitor wanting information. Are you a location based business or an online business?

If you're a location based business, where you work with your clients face-to-face, make sure they can figure out where you ARE. I know, I know — you want to work in cool destinations all over the world, so you chose to leave it off of your site. That way, it is like you are everywhere! Except, no. You're not.

People everywhere agree that not being able to find someone's location on their website is one of the more frustrating things, and that they will leave a website if it is difficult to locate.

You actually live in one location. People want to know that!

When I was still working as a photographer, I photographed destination weddings in Mexico, Belize, England, and around the USA.

All with the fact that I am located in Houston, Texas on my website. Some of my clients lived in Houston and chose to take me with them to their destination. Some lived in other locations and flew me in.

It has always been easy to find on my website where I live. Clients who want to work with you will fly you to their location or they will come to you.

Having your location on your website also gives people another way to connect with you. Maybe they lived in the same city at one point? Or they have always wanted to visit your area?

Humans, by nature, want to categorize other people. Talking about where you live gives them another data point for them. This information is also important so that they can then try to figure out when your work hours are so they don't call you at 5am in the morning if they live on the east coast of the United States and you're on the west coast, and they don't call you at midnight if you're in Australia and they are on the other side of the world.

Now they have figured out where you live, but how easy is it for them to contact you?

Do you have a contact form set up? What about an email address that is visible? Can I find your phone number?

If I was a member of the Oprah staff and wanted to feature your amazing awesomeness on TV, could I even get in touch with you? Or would I have to send up rocket flares to hopefully get your attention?

People. Don't make Oprah send up flares to reach you. Make it easy on her – and on everyone else who might want to work with you.

HOMEWORK

Put a "Contact" option in your menu bar, and on that page add all the juicy contact info you can come up with! And make sure you weave it throughout the content on your other pages too!

CHAPTER NINE

Creating Your Ideal Client Avatar

This is a great exercise for your business as a whole, not just for your blog. What can you tell me about who you are talking to with your marketing?

Years ago, I attended a workshop for wedding photographers and the speaker asked us to describe our ideal client. Most of the people he called on answered, "A bride looking for photojournalism style wedding photography." Or maybe "A couple getting married in Houston." Really vague, general answers.

My hand shot up in the air. I was giddy with excitement, ready to answer his question.

"My ideal wedding photography client is 27 to 37. While they are both active in planning, the bride contacts me first. She chose to have a career before getting married. She drives either Honda, Toyota or Mazda. She carries a Coach or Kate Spade purse, but she buys her t-shirts at Target.

She has no qualms spending money on luxury items – but likes to keep things simple if it is something she doesn't value much or is just a staple item. She has a college degree, and often additional education. She is likely marrying an engineer or a geek. Most of the time one if not both of them are from the Midwest, not Houston."

I continued, "They love good local restaurants (not chains), great wine, craft beer, and dinner with friends and family was one of their favorite activities. The person that she is marrying is very involved with their wedding planning, and will check in on my blog as well from time to time. There is a good chance that they will have a destination wedding."

The speaker was stunned. He did tours around the USA, and he said that in years he had never had someone describe their ideal client in that much detail. (Which was exactly what he was looking for in an answer.)

Knowing with that much clarity who I wanted to speak to made writing blog posts so much easier for me. You need to be authentic in what you share on your blog and social media, and especially be aware of what passions your ideal client or ideal blog reader shares with you. Coming from that place allows you to be you with no apologies!

That makes branding and marketing effortless.

Once I figured out who my ideal client was I discovered something else that was really important – I fit much of the description as well.

Ideal Client Avatar Exercise

How can you know what to say when you don't even know who you're talking to?

Grab a piece of paper, and let's dig in. Skip something if it really doesn't apply. I went with "she" for the pronoun, but if your ideal client is a man? Change it. If something doesn't fit? Skip it.

Here is what I want you to think about:

- Age
- Gender
- Hair color / eye color
- Location (city, state, country)
- Neighborhood (if in your city)
- Style of home – new or old? Urban, Suburban, Rural?
- Education Level (College? Masters? Doctorate?)
- Annual Income
- Career
- Married or single?
- When does she wear makeup, if she does at all?
- How does she normally style her hair?
- What are her interests?
- Does she have any hobbies?
- Any causes or things she is passionate about?

- Magazines she reads?
- Favorite books / movies / TV / music
- What other blogs does she read?
- Her favorite social media platforms
- Her favorite stores to shop at?
- What kind of car does she drive?
- How does she dress? Her favorite clothing item?
- Her favorite brand of purse?
- What is her favorite type of restaurant?
- Beer or wine? Coffee or tea?
- Mac or PC? iPhone, Android or Windows? iPad or Android tablet?
- Does she like to travel? Where does she go?
- Is her favorite Saturday night one out partying on the town? Or home with friends?
- Where will she share your website with her friends?
- What is her favorite social media platform?
- Where does she go to ask for recommendations?
- What is her favorite guilty pleasure?
- What are the luxuries she can't live without?
- Why is she reading your website?
- What will she want to buy from you?
- **MOST IMPORTANT: What are her pain points? What problem can you solve for her?**

Putting Together Your Ideal Client Avatar Profile

Do you feel like you are in their head now? Awesome! Your next step in creating your Ideal Client Avatar is to give her a name. Whatever you want. I want her to be so tangible to you that you feel like she could walk up to you on the street at any moment. You know her almost as well as your best friend.

Now, with every post you write, you can ask yourself what you want her to know. What do you want to say to her? What would she get out of the post? What problem are you solving for her with your content?

Creating an ideal client avatar helps you know exactly who you're talking to in your business & your blog.

The fastest way to clear writer's block? I think of it as if I'm writing a letter to my ideal client avatar. What can I tell her that will benefit her? Once I think of it from that angle, the words just flow.

Now that we know who you're writing for and why you're talking to her, we can create an editorial calendar full of content that will speak to her!

What if I Work With Several Different Types of Clients?

You might work with multiple types of clients if you photograph a variety of things. A senior girl in high school is different than the woman planning a wedding or a work at home mom that wants to book a session for her newborn. You can create an ideal client avatar for each of the people that you work with if it is easiest for you.

I often recommend looking at the clients to find the common ground. There most likely is personality traits among all of them that is similar; those senior girls will one day be the bride, who in turn will one day be planning a newborn session. Her music tastes, fashion sense, and everything else likely overlaps somewhat, and that overlap is what you can address in your posts.

When you look for the common ground, the traits that come up are almost always ones that you will identify with as well.

HOMEWORK

Take all the information you've gathered about your ideal client, and summarize it in to a brief. Tell me what her name is, describe her to me. Where does she live, what is she like, why is she reading your website.

Keep it to just one page if possible. If it helps you visualize her, find a photograph that matches your vision of her.

Be as detailed as possible.

When you're all done, tell us about your ideal client in the Business Brilliantly Facebook Group. You never know, maybe your next ideal client is there waiting for you?

CHAPTER TEN

The Power Of Evergreen Posts

You have this great idea for a post on Facebook. It is going to be wonderful, full of juicy tidbits and information. Everything that people that want to work with you or buy products from you should know.

STOP. Resist the temptation to post it on Facebook. Put it on your blog where it belongs!

Every day we think of wonderful things to say and share, and sprinkle them all across the internet on our various social media accounts. They will be seen for about 24 hours, if that, only to disappear and never be seen again. (Except if you truly wish they would disappear and never be seen again, because that random drunk tweet you decided to make at 2am? It won't ever completely go away.)

There is the big problem with social media - it has a very short shelf life. You need it to reach your audience, but it is a double-edged sword. Once you post it, it is gone.

Random tidbit: Did you know that Facebook actually hides posts from your Page if they don't get enough interaction? They even hide them from you!

However, if you post the great content on your blog? It can live on forever! This is why we call it Evergreen Content.

Your blog is like a giant library of your knowledge. Everything that makes you an expert can be contained here, all in one place. Then you can refer back to it over and over again - post a link to it in a Facebook Group. Share it over on LinkedIn. Pin it to Pinterest. Send it to a client over email. Tell your friends about it in a conversation.

That content can live on and on.

Now, when people come to your website they can browse through different things that you have written over time. If there is a post that interests them, they can follow links to similar posts if you're using a related posts plugin, or manually adding related posts to your current ones. They can find it if they go through categories or tags on your website.

Your content will work for you, instead of the 48 hour shelf life of a Facebook post.

HOMEWORK

Go through your posts that you've already written and make sure that they are Evergreen. (If you mention a special or a sale in them that has already passed, remove the details if possible.)

Write one blog post this week that is something that you find that you share with everyone about your business. Is there a story you always tell new clients? Or tips that they should know about your products?

Creating Your Content Plan For Your Blog – The Editorial Calendar

The concept of Editorial Calendars for blogs is inspired by the magazine industry. They guide the flow of the publication year-round. For magazines, they are publicly available; you can look them up online and find out well in advance the theme that they will be covering in upcoming issues.

For example, you can view the editorial calendar for Vogue online at http://www.condenast.com/brands/vogue/media-kit/print/calendar. Why do they post their editorial calendar online? Because that way, if you're an advertiser in their magazine, you know what is coming up and you can plan out your ad campaigns.

Think of any magazine that you like and look them up; you will most likely find their Editorial Calendar online.

Adapting this concept for our use is one of the best things that we can do to create an engaging blog that our readers will want to return to time and time again.

Why You Need an Editorial Calendar For Your Blog

You don't need to share your calendar online for everyone to see, but you do need to have a plan for your blog. Creating an editorial calendar will make things go so much smoother for you when it comes to blogging!

Think about it, no more stumbling along and wondering what to write. You can look at your calendar and just go from there!

What stories do you want to share with your future clients so that they will be interested in hiring you? What are the stories you want them to pass on to other people about you? How will you connect with them?

Having an editorial calendar takes the pressure off of you when it comes time to write a blog post, which is the main reason why you need one. Having an Editorial Calendar means you have a plan.

You know what you want to say (at least from a high level), and you know WHY you want to say it. You know how it fits with your marketing plan. Your blog isn't just a gaping void of frustration for you, one where simply opening up the post box is terrifying. Instead, you can use it to take you where you want to go.

The editorial calendar? That is at the heart of it!

Some people call this a content or marketing calendar. To me, they are the same thing – and I prefer to use the term editorial calendar. Either one works — the most important thing is to have one!

HOMEWORK

Start thinking about what you want to post about on your blog. Are there series you want to create? Weekly or monthly features you want to include? What are some of the things that your ideal client is interested in?

Do you want to have monthly themes? How will it tie in to your own marketing plan. Make a list and you'll be ready to roll!

When you're all done with your list, share some of your ideas or lightbulb moments with us in the Business, Brilliantly Facebook Group.

Interested in learning even more about how to create your Editorial Calendar? I have a free bonus PDF, my gift to you, that you can download at:

http://christinetremoulet.com/editorial-calendar-gift

CHAPTER TWELVE

Tips For Planning Out Your Blog Content

Before we dive in to how create your Editorial Calendar, we need to discuss the most frequent source of resistance on this topic: you don't like to write on demand. You would much rather write when the mood strikes, when you're feeling passionate about a topic, when you feel inspired.

I get you. I feel exactly the same way.

Even if you feel this way, the Editorial Calendar will make blogging so much easier for you. It is the key to busting through writer's block. Yes, really even for those of us that don't like to write on demand.

How you create your calendar is completely up to you. I am going to share here how I create mine and give you ideas of alternative ways to do it. Just remember, we are doing this to make blogging easier. Or, as my Dad always says, you need to follow the 6 Ps. Pre-Planning Prevents

Piss-Poor Performance. If you want your blog humming along and your readers coming back for more? You need a plan.

How Often Should You Blog?

Your first decision is how many times a week do you want to post on your website. This question is debated time & time again. My take on it? You should blog as often as you can create quality content that is interesting for your readers. For some people that is 4 times a week, and for others that is once a week. Once a week is what I recommend to start with, and you can go up from there. That is only 52 posts in a year. 52! You've got this.

Choose which day of the week that you would like your posts to go out on and at what time. I often get a burst of writing inspiration on Wednesday or Thursday, so my posts normally go live on Thursday afternoon.

Study your site's stats to see which days you have the most traffic or at which time, and focus on that time for your own calendar if you would like.

Use Your Calendar

Review when any marketing campaigns are coming up. Is your business is seasonal with sales around holidays? Know when posts relating to that need to be published. Do you have any launches planned for the year? Great, mark them on there as well.

Do you know when you need to be writing your blog posts for an upcoming sale? Let's say you're a photographer and you do a special photo session for Christmas cards every year. You need to have all of the products in people's hands no later than December 1st.

Working backwards, that means that you need to have all of your ordering sessions by November 15th; you need to be done taking the photos by November 1st; and you want 6 weeks for the sessions to take place. That means your sessions will start in mid-September.

Before I had an Editorial Calendar planned out, I'd often wait until late September to start talking about the holiday sessions on my blog, when I actually should have started mentioning them in August or early September to get clients booked in time for me to be able to deliver the products on time!

You do not have to plan out your full year of posts all at once; planning out 3-6 months will give you time to measure how people respond to your content. Just be sure to be mindful of holidays and anything else important.

Keeping Post Ideas Organized

Follow these steps and you'll add rocket fuel to your writing time.

(1)   Keep a running brain dump list of post ideas to refer to in Evernote, OneNote, or something similar on your mobile device. Having it with you at all times makes it easier to add to when you feel inspired.

(2)   Notecards - write one post idea per notecard, and add notes on the back for when you're ready to write. Get tactile, move them around as you plan out your upcoming posts, making it easier to group them in sets, series, or around important calendar dates. Stuck needing something to write about? Pull a card and challenge yourself.

(3)   Use Plugins to see your calendar online such as CoSchedule (http://coschedule.com/r/11203) and Word-Press Editorial Calendar (free in the WordPress Plugin Directory) are both great options.

Not on WordPress? You can still use CoSchedule to plan out your social media broadcasts of your posts by logging in to the CoSchedule site.

Have a Variety Of Topics?

Sometimes, people want to write about a variety of topics on their blog. This allows people to have a chance to get to know you better; after all, you are more than your business. There is no right or wrong way to do this, and you are the common thread throughout all of your posts.

One idea to consider is that a certain day of the week is when you post about a certain topic. That way, it will be more expected by your readers.

HOMEWORK

Decide how you want to organize your blog post ideas, and if you want to dig into one of the recommended plugins, check those out as well. Make sure you plan out your most important marketing dates, so you can take advantage of them and not blog at the last minute!

Don't forget to download the free bonus PDF, my gift to you to help you with this, by visiting here:
http://christinetremoulet.com/editorial-calendar-gift

CHAPTER THIRTEEN

Using Google Analytics To Build Your Blog Calendar

When you are working on your Editorial Calendar for your blog, one more great place to look for inspiration is at what Google Analytics has to tell you.

Google Analytics is full of data. TONS of information. And … I have to confess I used to always get lost in there. (Ok, sometimes I still get lost in there!)

Today I'll share with you where to go to find the highest traffic pages on your website in Analytics. That is one of my favorite things to check out because it helps me lay the foundation for the ever wonderful and important Editorial Calendar!

Analytics tells me what has resonated with people, what you are reading, what you are likely sharing (if traffic is up for a post) and what you find engaging.

If it is content you enjoy as a reader, I want to write more about it.

Especially if I have more to say about it, or if I can approach it from another angle without being redundant. If it is something I love to talk about but the engagement wasn't so great, it gives me a chance to review it again, see what I might have missed, or find ways to continue to talk about it that might be more interesting or that Google might pick up on for SEO.

To find this data in Google Analytics, you want to log in to your account. From there, on the left menu bar, look for the section named

"Behavior". Random name, which is probably why I missed it for so long!

Once you select Behavior, the Overview screen will show you the top 10 posts on your website. If one is titled "/" that means it is your home page. For most people, I'd expect that to be the most trafficked page on your site – unless you have a static page and a blog. Then your blog will be even higher.

Looking at Behavior >> Site Content >> All Pages will also provide you with this information, along with additional data. (On the iPhone Google Analytics app it is simply Behavior >> All Pages.)

You can select the date range for the data you want to view – I like to view "Month" to get an overview of what is popular.

Now if you're ever stuck thinking of what to write about for your ideal client, you can use the power of Google Analytics to see what they are already reading the most often, and if it resonates for you? Share more of that!

HOMEWORK

Go play around with your Google Analytics! If you haven't had a chance to install it yet, go back to the chapter on adding it to your website.

Come share your most popular posts in the Business Brilliantly Facebook Group.

Five Simple Tips To Make Lazy Readers Stay On Your Blog

"The minute it's not easy, lazy people will flee. And everyone is lazy sometimes."– Seth Godin

Go to your blog. We need to look at some things, because we have to help the lazy people out. You want them to stay, you don't want them to flee, right?

1. How fast does your website load? People aren't just lazy, they have no patience as well. You need your blog to load fast. Look at the graphics you have on your page – are you uploading high resolution images to your blog and then requiring it to resize them small?

Do you have 40 buttons in the sidebar that are all loading from different sources (besides your server)? Does every blog post have 20 images, and the home page of your blog has 10 posts on it?

You get the point – those images are slowing you down. Make them smaller and web-friendly and make your blog faster. Consider only loading 5 posts on your site, not 10. Speed it up!

2. Where do you want me to go? Look at the navigation on your site. First of all, can you find it? Is there a menu bar on the top, or a menu on the sidebar? How do you go from post to post? How do you learn more about you? Can you find your pricing?

How about to contact you? Whatever you want people to do next when they come to your site – make that thing EASY to find.

3. Can you read the fonts? If I was on a 27″ monitor, would the fonts on your site be teeny-tiny small? How is the contrast to read?

I know you love that super light blue font on a white background, and it matches your branding – but if you can't read it, what good is it doing? (Believe it or not, people with visual impairments do read the internet!)

Help people out. Bump up the contrast, and make sure the fonts are not too small.

4. Scroll, scroll, scroll How long do you have to scroll just to find the very first blog post? Do you lose patience with all the scrolling?

5. Can you get more of this goodness? Ok, they came, they saw, they want MORE. Yay! Is there a way that you can easily sign up for your email list? How hard is that to find? Do you send out emails with every new blog post? Once a month? Once a whenever-you-get-around-to-it?

Do you have links at the bottom of each post to other posts that your readers might like? This feature is included in some themes, or you can use a plugin to automatically generate them. If you prefer, you can also link to them manually, choosing which ones you want to send people to when they leave the current post. This helps keep people on your site longer, so they can learn even more about you.

These quick little fixes will help you out when your readers have the lazies. The more you make it easy for them, the longer they will stick around!

And sticking around is key to a successful, thriving business.

HOMEWORK

Using the above questions, see how your site is doing. Make any changes that you can, and then create a "wish list" for improvements you need to outsource to a virtual assistant or perhaps to a designer/developer.

CHAPTER FIFTEEN

Automate Your Blogging And Social Sharing

Every time you write a blog post, it isn't just about writing the post. Sometimes, that feels like that is the easiest part.

Remember, the blog is the center of your social media universe. Once you are done, you need to broadcast it all over social media so that people know to come back and check it out.

When you are creating content, the majority of it will be evergreen posts. These are posts that never expire. Think of them like your own library of information; posts that answer clients frequently asked questions, provide them with timeless tips, or anything else that doesn't have a date on it. (For example, a post about an upcoming sale you are having is not evergreen. You do not want to keep sharing it after the sale is over.)

Recycle Your Content Wisely

Evergreen posts can be shared on social media again and again. It is acceptable on social media to share them again weekly or monthly for as long as you want. Creating content once, and using it many times. Keeping up with all of that manually is far too time consuming. You have better things to do.

We need to automate it all so that you can do it all at once and be done with it!

My Favorite Tools For Automating Your Blog

There are a number of tools out there that you can use to schedule social sharing on Twitter, Facebook, LinkedIn, Pinterest, and Instagram. The list of companies that offer options for doing this is always growing. These are the tools I am using right now, and the combination of them works very well for me.

Look around though and see what is best for you and choose what parts you want to automate and what features interest you. Most companies offer a trial period to test out their products..

CoSchedule: (Paid, WordPress Plugin available, Stand-alone option for Squarespace) After I have set up my blog post, I go to the CoSchedule section of my WordPress post. Since I have the plugin installed, I do not have to even leave WordPress to schedule future posts. I set up my post to be shared immediately with Twitter, Facebook, LinkedIn, and any Facebook Groups that I administer that the post applies to.

Once I do that, I choose when in the future I want the post to go out online: the next day, next week, in a month, or on a custom date. There is no limit to how many times I can schedule it.

CoSchedule shares on their blog the research that they have done; blog posts get engagement on Twitter being shared nearly daily, sometimes multiple times during the day. Sharing repeatedly on Facebook pages is also an option.

Know your audience and what posting schedule will increase your engagement on your blog by running your own tests. Personally, I share on Twitter for the first few days, and then again a week later, a month later, three months later, and six months later. I share the same post on Facebook again a month later, three months later, and six months later. I vary the comments that go out with the post so that they don't all look the same.

I love that I can quickly and easily do this all on one place, and that I can view a calendar within my WordPress site to see all of my upcoming blog posts and social media posts in one place.

You can also schedule Tweets, Facebook status updates (personal and business), Facebook Group (administrator only) and LinkedIn updates all without them being related to a particular blog post.

Additionally, you can use Buffer with CoSchedule to connect to Google+ pages, and you can use Bit.ly to track stats on the things you share online.

They continue to add and update features available, including a new headline analysis tool to determine if your headlines are well written.

WordPress is not required for use; you can use Co-Schedule to schedule your social media for other blogging platforms.

Learn more about CoSchedule and test it out here: http://ChristineTremoulet.com/CoSchedule

Tailwind: (Paid, Google Chrome browser plugin available) My next step is to head over to the Tailwind site to schedule my Pinterest posts for the blog post. Pinterest is a great source of traffic for me, and pinning content is the best way to help people there find you. With the Tailwind app, I can schedule when pins will go out in the future, spread out so that people are not flooded with my Pinterest pin-fests. You define the schedule that is right for you and your audience.

Every 30 days I repin my own site content pins. I know that sounds like a lot, but this is the same principle as sharing your content repeated to Twitter and Facebook. A pin has a limited life, and for my evergreen content I want people to see it again.

As long as you are pinning other people's content between pins of your own, which is easy using their Chrome plugin to pin anything you see online, it will help to bring you more traffic. There is an option for me to see all of the pins I have scheduled in the past and repin those - it just takes an extra step. You can learn more about the latest features of Tailwind here: http://tailwindapp.com/i/christinebpc

Sendible: (Paid) Overlaps in features with a number of things that CoSchedule and Tailwind can do, and it has the ability to recycle your pins. I personally choose the CoSchedule and Tailwind option, but you could do a trial of Sendible to see which one you like best. I found their interface to be more complex than what I was looking for when I was setting up my automation process.

If you like to have a lot of stats, the ability to do everything in one place, and many other features, Sendible may be something you want to consider. http://sendible.com/

Onlypult: (Paid) My preferred Instagram scheduler because it publishes your posts for you. You can see a schedule of pins that you have coming up, and when it is time for them to go live you do not have to do anything, it is all taken care of for you. I do not schedule all of my Instagram posts because, for me, I like to go in to Instagram and see the latest ones and interact with the community there. I schedule daily motivational quotes, photographs from my travel adventures, and graphics relating to any promotions I am doing.

Onlypult is also great if you are looking for analytics on your Instagram account, if you really want to be able to post from the web instead of a mobile device, and if you manage multiple Instagram accounts. You can learn more about Onlypult and the services they offer here: https://onlypult.com

Latergram.me: (Free or Paid) Latergramme is another Instagram scheduler. They offer a web interface and an iPhone app; you will have to swipe to post with the web app on your phone when it is time to send out a post. Posts do not go live without your interaction. Learn more at http://latergram.me

Schedugr.am: (Paid) offers similar features to OnlyPult, including posting for you so that you do not have to interact once you have scheduled a post. If you manage multiple accounts it costs more. You can learn more about this at http://Schedugr.am

Automation Isn't Free

Most of these services are not free, so you will need to decide if paying for them is worth the time that you will save. The convenience and ease of use for my team is worth the monthly or annual fees for my business. I did not want to have to spend time thinking about maintaining a presence on all of these accounts at the same time. This allows me to batch process my work.

If you prefer to do things manually, you can chart out your social media schedule on paper, and then make the status updates throughout the day.

HOMEWORK

Decide what you need to automate, and how much work that would take off your plate for bigger, and better uses of your time. Then invest in whichever automation tool that appeals to you. Automation is life changing!

Pinning For Inspiration

Pinterest is a treasure-trove of inspiration for me most of the time, although sometimes it is easy to get lost in all of the great things that you can find there! If you use it wisely though, you can benefit from it to grow your blog.

Busting Through Writer's Block

Keep a secret pin board of topics that you find inspiring and that are things you will want to talk about someday myself. Think of it as your own tickler file, things that you can flip though when you are stuck. I personally make it a rule not to open and read the posts, because I don't want to accidentally say the exact same thing that they did.

Just browsing through the titles is enough to inspire me to plow through and get a post done.

This is also a great way to study what titles get people's interest and what doesn't so that you can create your own enticing post titles for your blog.

Branding & Marketing Inspiration

Create a pin board of things that you visually love. It can be photographs that make you happy, logos that you think are beautiful, business cards that you wish that you had. Do not limit yourself on what you have on this board!

Mine has everything from my favorite Pendleton blanket that I own to pieces of furniture, even photographs of full rooms. Clothing that is a style that I would wear. My favorite places I have traveled, and places that I want to visit someday. Anything that feels like a visual representation of me and makes my heart sing.

Once you gather all of these various items together, you can look at the collection as a whole and often spot very obvious trends. You will notice colors that are repeated or that jump out at you. Textures. Overall aesthetics.

This is a great way to find your style and determine what your website should look like to represent you, determine what colors you should use in your marketing materials, and get inspiration for designing templates for your social media graphics.

If you're working with a designer, you can provide them with your board. If you're doing your site yourself, you will find your direction much easier once you can see what you love.

Find Quotables

I love a good quote, and I share them often on Instagram. I've kept a journal of quotes over the years, yet sometimes I find myself looking for something special. Pinterest is full of quotes! Don't just take the ones that you see there, which would be copyright infringement; instead create your own with your unique branding and style! I use my personal photographs or a solid backdrop to display them on Instagram & Pinterest.

Share Your Site with the World

Don't forget to pin your own posts! For each post that you write, you will want to create a Pinterest friendly graphic so that you and your readers can share it over there.

Vertical images are preferred as the long, tall ones will take up the most visual space and be more appealing. Make your graphics 735 pixels wide; the length of them is up to you, but they will be cut off in the Pinterest display if they are too long. Canva.com recommends a size of 735x1102.

Skip the hashtags on Pinterest; they don't use them, and you could be penalized and your posts might not be displayed.

Note: all of the other social media prefers square or horizontal graphics; you might want to design two graphics for each post, that way you can share the right image size on the social media account. If you use Canva for Work this process is super easy to set up graphics for other social media networks based on a graphic you've already created.

Find Your Most Popular Posts on Pinterest

Ever wonder what your most popular posts on Pinterest are? Visit http://Pinterest.com/source/*yourdomain.com* to see what pins link back to your domain.

HOMEWORK

Have some fun pinning for inspiration! If you use a service like Tailwind or Sendible, fill up your queue with posts that your ideal client would love as well.

Look up the pins from your site. Are there any blog posts that you should make Pinterest-friendly graphics for? Do they need a refresh to be more consistent with your brand? Pick five posts to make fresh and pin the new graphics.

If you need help crafting creative graphics, you can use Canva or PicMonkey on your computer or tablet, or text apps like WordSwag and Phonto on your mobile device.

CHAPTER SEVENTEEN

Do You Really Need A Blog Redesign?

I have a confession: I set myself up to fail some days. I mean, this is never an intentional decision – I do not LIKE to fail – but I still self-sabotage a bit some days.

You know what I mean?

I've been trying to be more mindful when it happens, so that I can then analyze if what I think is a problem in my business really is one, or if I'm just blocking myself.

My most recent blockade? Thinking I had to completely redesign my website.

My website, as it was, was perfectly fine. It looked good, and it functioned great. No problems there. My problem was it didn't look JUST RIGHT.

I've been down this road before. Matter of fact, I recently read one of my first blog posts back in May, 2000 and I mentioned in the post that I needed to merge sites, and it really needed a different design. 16+ years later, and the story is still the same.

When you own a house, if you didn't like the color on the walls in the living room, would you tear the walls down and build a completely new house instead of going and buying a can of paint?

This is not a realistic response.

I have never caught before that I do this to myself. This time? I had to make myself stop and think about it. Dig in. What was really happening here?

What Is The Pattern When I Create This Block For Myself?

Every time I use this excuse to block myself from moving forward in my business, I do the exact same thing — I start to hunt for a new website theme. I spend hours researching options. Making lists. I then end up messaging my (very patient) friends to get their feedback on all the themes I have select.

After that, I sometimes even ask on Facebook for feedback from more people.

The reality? When this happens I'm operating from a place of fear. I'm afraid to be seen, to be heard. I'm afraid that no one will notice me. I'm looking for someone to just tell me what to do.

I want to make it easier on myself. To make it so that I do not have to decide. I hate making decisions. Simultaneously, I insist on controlling the decision. Yes, it is a little confusing for me too.

Processing Through My Block

One thing I know about myself is that I work things out by talking through them. So I end up weighing things; voicing my opinions on what is not good for me, or offering up alternatives that are good for me. All help me to articulate what I'm looking for in reality.

This time, my husband Mike suggested that I draw out what I wanted. Pen to paper, I made a sketch of what I had in mind. That helped me start to get focused; it gave me a super clear direction to go.

At that point, I gave myself two days to find a theme I liked. I narrowed it down to three, and then wrote to the support teams about them to ask if certain features existed.

Then it hit me – finding images and writing copy was going to take me a lot of time. Logical as can be, but something I had not thought of until that very moment. Pictures and words don't magically appear on your website, after all.

I realized I did not have time for that. It was not serving my business or myself.

What the hell was I doing?

I looked back at the sketch I had made. An idea finally started to come together, and I realized that just spending an hour or two on my current website would allow me create something quite close to my original vision, without that much of a time investment.

There was one more thing that was even more important though: changing my website design was not going to impact the bottom line of my business profits.

Not one bit.

This is the lie that we tell ourselves! We say that if only our website design was perfect, or if our copy on our site was dreamy, then our businesses could be great.

Know what makes your business great? Getting it out there and in front of your ideal people.

Your ideal clients? They don't care which theme you are using! They don't care if your copy is perfectly tweaked and super dreamy! They do not care if unicorns fly overhead and drop glitter sparkle dust all over everything. That is not why they choose to read your website with you!

Your Profit Margin And Your Website

Now if your website totally sucks and you wouldn't ever want anyone to see it or to know it belongs to you? Yes. Then you should redesign it. That was not the case for me. My website was solidly in a state of "Very MuchGood Enough."

It makes more sense for my business to make money with what I have and then down the road hire a designer to make my perfect dream a reality. I am NOT generating income for my business when I am working on my website. That does not serve me or my business.

Remember: if your business isn't making a profit, it isn't a business. It is an expensive hobby.

I've pulled out the website block in my own business. Yes, I spent 2-3 hours moving some things around, changing out my header, adding things to my sidebar. I have a few more changes I would like to make still, but they will happen when they happen – my business is not going to wait on them.

I'm going to move forward. I'm going to focus more on sending people here, on working with them, on providing solutions to their problems, and on making money.

Your blog will help you dominate your market. It is the content on your site that helps you do that, first and foremost. Focus where it matters first.

What Are Your Road Blocks? Why Did You Put Them There?

Do you have something standing in your way? Keeping you from moving forward? Is it a flying unicorn with glitter sparkles excuse of what you need to have … and if only you had THAT thing then surely you would be successful?

What is that unicorn really hiding from you? What blocks are you putting in your own way?

HOMEWORK

Think about where you typically get hung up in your own business. It could be on branding, or site design. Maybe you're getting stuck on your business name, or pricing. Whatever it is? By letting yourself get dragged into time wasters instead of moving forward, you're wasting time you could be connecting with those beautiful, awesome clients just waiting for you!

Care to share where you get stuck? Let's talk about it in the Business Brilliantly Facebook group.

CHAPTER EIGHTEEN

Getting Legal With Your Blog: Disclaimers, Disclosures & Photography

Ugh. The legal stuff. No one wants to think about it, but if you don't? Your business can end up in a lot of hot water!

There are many different things that you need to do for your business to make it be legal - register with the government, get a business license, whatever is required in your area. Did you realize that there are things that you need to do to make your blog legal as well?

DISCLAIMER: I am not a lawyer. This should not be construed in ANY WAY as legal or other advice. Please seek legal counsel to advise on your own situation.

The Federal Trade Commission & Disclaimers

If you are an American, this one applies to you. The Federal Trade Commission has guidelines about what you do with your blog and social media accounts. These rules impact everything from contests for your own business to sponsored posts for other businesses. One of the most important to note is that you must disclose any time you are reviewing a product that you were given for free in exchange for a review or that you were paid for the review.

How you disclose, where you disclose - all of it. It is your responsibility to keep up with these guidelines. The majority apply if you are reviewing products for a profit in some form for yourself.

You can find the official guidelines online here: https://www.ftc.gov/sites/default/files /attachments/press-releases/ftc-staffrevises-online-advertising-disclosureguidelines/130312dotcomdisclosures. pdf

This additional page from the FTC has more helpful information on how to handle the guidelines - https://www.ftc.gov/tipsadvice/businesscenter/guidance/ftcs-endorsementguides-what-people-are-asking

If you're not an American, you need to check to see if your government has similar rules & regulations.

Terms Of Service & Your Privacy Policy

These are the guidelines that people that use your site must abide by while visiting, and they detail what they can expect from you. You're defining the rights of your visitors and what you will do with the data that they provide to you. You may not be the next Facebook, yet you still need to include these.

Rachel Brenke, the lawyer behind TheLawTog and BlogLegally, offers great templates to help you with creating your Terms of Service and Privacy Policy, along with contracts and forms for other aspects of your business. Be sure to visit her shop for lawyer drafted templates: http://ChristineTremoulet.com/ bloglegally

Please note: If you purchase a template from Rachel Brenke (or anyone else), have your lawyer review it to make sure it complies with your local laws. Having this starting point will still save you a great deal of money.

Edit legal documents on your own with caution; lawyers have to go to school for this because terms that look simple to us often have a more complex meaning in the eyes of the law. Removing a critical word could have very major implications for you if you end up in legal hot water.

Photographs For Your Website

The easiest way to guarantee that you can legally use a photograph on your website is to take the picture yourself.

The minute your finger leaves the shutter, you own the copyright on the image. There are still laws governing your rights to use the likeness of a person and art for commercial use, model releases, what permission you need, and so forth. Knowing that you own the photograph is the best starting point.

Sometimes, you need a photograph that you can't take.

Maybe the subject matter isn't near your location, you don't have a model, or even that you don't feel you're a good photographer. Whatever the case may be, when you go online to find an image to use for your blog? Be sure it is one where you have rights to use it for commercial use. Do not start with doing a Google Image Search and assume that those are legal for you to use!

Those images are almost always protected by copyright by the owner, and they are not free for you to use. In order to avoid breaking any laws and suddenly receiving a takedown notice (or worse, your website provider pulling your site offline), make sure you get your images from a source that has licensing information clearly listed and allows for commercial use. (In other words? Don't just go and take photographs off of someone else's website. Save yourself the headache.)

Paid Stock Photography

Creative Market: In addition to their photos section, Creative Market has many amazing finds for building your website. So many pretty things!

https://creativemarket.com/photos?u =christinetremoulet

Stocksy: Some of the most gorgeous stock photography around; worth the price if you want a unique look! http://stocksy.com

Creative Commons Licensed Photographs

The Creative Commons is a nonprofit organization founded in 2001. They created licenses as a way for people to easily denote that their images could be used for a number of purposes. Think of it as "Some Rights Reserved."

Flickr makes it easy for users to add a Creative Commons license (CC) to their photographs, as does the site 500px. To find Creative Commons Licensed photos on Flickr, you can use a service that searches through their files. I use http://compfight.com and set the Creative Commons License option to "Commercial" in the left sidebar.

To find Creative Commons Licensed photos on 500px, visit https://500px.com/creativecommons

Be sure to credit the original source as required by the CC terms.

Free Stock Photography

The following sources offer free stock photography for commercial use. Be sure to view their Terms of Service to make sure you comply with their guidelines for use of the images.

Pixabay: No membership required, although it is free & helpful for downloading photographs. Easy to use and one of the best resources around. http://Pixabay.com

Death to Stock Photography: Supply your email address and once a month they will send you large, beautiful stock photographs. Learn more about them here: http://deathtothestockphoto.com

Cupcake: Jonas Nilsson Lee offers his photographs up for free use under the Creative Commons CC0 License. You can copy, modify, distribute and perform the work, even for commercial purposes, all without asking for permission. (These are not food photographs, it is just the name of the site.) http://cupcake.nilssonlee.se/

Free Nature Stock Royalty-free Nature Stock Photos: free to use any way you want, by Adrian Pelletier. http://freenaturestock.com/

Jay Mantri: Jay is another photographer with a diverse range of photographs that are offered with a CC0 license, free for you to use. http://jaymantri.com/

Gratisography: Free high-resolution pictures you can use on your personal and commercial projects. All pictures were photographed by Ryan McGuire and free of copyright restrictions. http://www.gratisography.com

Pexels: Beautiful, large, free high-resolution images. http://www.pexels.com

Unsplash: Some of my personal favorite high-resolution, free for commercial use images; these photographs are very popular and seen on many websites. https://unsplash.com

HOMEWORK

Make sure that you're covered with appropriate terms of service, and legal photos (either paid or properly credited) on your site.

Any other stock photography sites that you love? Advice for legal coverage? We'd love to hear about them in the Business Brilliantly group!

CHAPTER NINETEEN

Bringing Benefits To Your Readers

When you write a blog post, where do you find yourself starting at? Do you talk initially about yourself, or the person reading your site? Do you launch right in to your story, or do you invite your reader in to the conversation? Do you make the story flow around them?

To turn your readers from potential clients in to raving fans, create from a place of giving. Approach your website with an attitude of service, of helping people get exactly what THEY need.

Your Key To Unlocking This Valuable Content? Remember Your Purpose.

What benefits can you share with your readers? What do you have that can make them better people, more profitable, help them become healthier, whatever it is that you do what are the benefits to working with you?

When you are busy growing your business, it is so easy to be focused on what you need. You need to build your website, create a social media presence, set up your shopping cart, Facebook ads, find clients, and start to bring in a profit. It becomes all about you, and it is hard to make it about them.

Look at the content of your website.

How often are you saying "I" or "We"? Now how often are you saying "You"?

Did you realize that the word "you" is one of the most persuasive words in the English language. The more you can say it in your website copy, the more people will want to read.

Add in the other four most persuasive words in your calls to action on your site: Free, Because, Instantly, and New. (Read more on why they are persuasive, at Copyblogger at http://www.copyblogger.com/persuasive-copywriting-words/)

Please know, I'm not saying that you can't talk about yourself here. You can - because we truly want to connect with you and get to know you! Bring me along for the conversation though.

Don't just tell me how great you are tell me how you are going to MAKE me great.

When you do that? I can't help but come back for more!

People Buy Benefits, Not Features

People care about features only after they want to buy the benefits.

Any time you're unsure if something is a benefit or a feature, try to look at it from the perspective of your client. What will they get out of it? What will they gain? How will you solve their problem?

If a statement answers the "What's in it for me?" question for your clients, it is a benefit. If it you can ask "So what?" as a response? It is a feature.

For example:

I offer a course on Business Brilliantly. It is 30 days long. We've answered "So what?" 30 days of content. Boom! That is a feature!

I offer a course on Business Brilliantly. It will help you dominate your market by standing out as authentically you. This answers "What's in it for me?" You will stand out in your crowded market. Boom! That is a benefit!

HOMEWORK

Write out a list 5-10 benefits that you can think of that you provide through your services or products. (You can write more than that, but 5-10 is a great start!) Keep in mind, the benefits have to be things that help the buyer - they cannot be features.

Remember: if your response is, "So what?" it is a feature. If it can answer the "What's in it for me?" question, it is a benefit.

Once you have listed the benefits, you can now write a blog post, or several, around each benefit that you have listed. Content your readers will instantly love and want to share with others!

How can you change YOUR conversation to the benefits, not the features, for your clients? Tell us in the group.

CHAPTER TWENTY

Seven Essential Steps To Making A Profit From Your Blog

We all tell ourselves stories about how if our site looks perfect, or just like our competition's site, then and only then will our businesses finally take off.

If you have been following along with the steps we have covered up to this point, you have all of the most critical things to make your site successful; some of these are a recap, and some of these you need to spend time thinking about.

Here is what REALLY matters when it comes to making money with your blog & website - far more than the design itself - and the last one is the one I find many people skip:

Is your site functional? Do the graphics load, is it fast, and are the links working? Fix anything that is broken.

Hire someone to help if needed, you don't have to do it yourself. There are only so many hours in the day. Once you have these essentials fixed, move on down the list.

Can your clients find what they are looking for easily? If I start on your home page, can I find out more about you? Can I find what services or products you are offering? Do you use terms that are familiar to me for your navigation, or are you using phrases that you felt were charming and creative, but leave me hunting all over for the information that I need? Yeah. Don't make it hard for me. Think about the path you want me to take, and then set your navigation on your site up to match it. Use dropdowns where needed to keep it from being too cluttered. Ditch pages that are not truly essential.

Are your offerings clearly worded and easy me to understand? If you want me to hire you, I need to know what you're selling, especially the benefits of why I should have it. Give me all the information I need to make a decision! Don't spend too much time on making the words all perfectly fancy and optimized to the hilt at first; once you are making some money, you can hire an expert to do these things for you. Just get me to where I know what you have, how much it costs (if you want to share that), and how I can get it. Which brings me to…

Is there a way to contact you if I want to know more? If you're putting all sorts of great stuff on your website, awesome. Do I have to hunt you down to talk to you though? If it isn't easy, I'll just move on to the next website on my list. Keep it simple!

Are you providing valuable content that entices me to come back for more? Are you sharing your stories? Your wisdom? Your knowledge? WRITE A BLOG POST AL-READY! You are the expert here! You need to tell me that. You can have the most basic, minimalist website in the world, and if the content is great, I will return over and over again. Content is Queen! (I know some people say Content is King, but women use thousands more words in a day than men according to research, so that makes Content the Queen in my book!)

Do you have a way for me to get on your email list so that you can reach me in the future? You may say that pop-ups are annoying, but the facts prove that they work. I grew my email list 150% the first month that I installed the easy to use PopUpAlly Pro plugin on to my website (http://ChristineTremoulet.com/PopUpAllyPro). People joined that were engaged, and kept coming back for more. PopUpAlly Pro offers options for polite popups - ones that only display as someone goes to exit the site, for example. Even if you don't have a pop-up on your website, have links to a list somewhere. Give them a chance to stay in touch.

THE BIGGEST ONE: Are you actually telling people that you have a business and that they can work with you? This is really, really big. Are you telling me that I can hire you? Are there calls to action throughout your site? Get on that.

Start speaking up and actually telling me why I should work with you. I can't hear what you don't say!

HOMEWORK

Review your site and make sure things are easy to find. Ask friends to look through your website and tell you if they can find where you are located. Get them on the phone and ask them to tell you about your products or services, based only on what they see online.

Make sure that you have a call to action, encouraging me to join your email list or consider a related product that you offer throughout your site. I can't buy what I don't know about.

Invite people to check out your site via social media, and tag #BusinessBrilliantly so we can as well!

CHAPTER TWENTY-ONE

Is Your Site Mobile Friendly?

Here is an interesting fact for you — according to Pew Research, in May 2013, *"34% of cell internet users go online mostly using their phones, and not using some other device such as a desktop or laptop computer."* (Pew Research Internet Project: Mobile Technology Fact Sheet, http://www.pewinternet.org/factsheets/mobile-technology-factsheet/)

34% of people online were primarily using a mobile device to get online in early 2013. Just imagine what that number is up to today!

Looking through my Google Analytics stats for 4 different websites, my numbers support this – over 40% of my site visitors are on mobile devices.

Yet I can't tell you how many times I've heard people say that they don't care what their website looks like on a phone, it is meant to be experienced on a computer.

Guess what? You don't get to decide how people view your site. You need it to be mobile friendly if you want to stay in the game.

Add to that the fact that Google has added how mobile-friendly your website in as a factor in how they rank you with SEO. They will rank mobile-friendly sites higher, because of how many mobile users are online. This change could impact people's websites more than Google's Penguin and Panda updates combined, it is that big of a deal.

Not sure if your site is mobile friendly? Use the Google Webmaster's Mobile-Friendly Test. It will tell you if Google sees your site that way. https://www.google.com/webmasters/tools/mobile-friendly/

HOMEWORK

Today's task is to grab your phone and look at your site. Closely. If you were visiting it for the first time, could you find what you want to know? Could you zoom in on the page to read the text? Could you find contact information to hire you? How is the menu to navigate? Can you go from section to section?

Bonus points if you can get your hands on another type of mobile device to check it there. If you use an iPhone, get access to an Android. Check it on a phone and a tablet or two. Look at it as many ways as possible.

Make sure the experience is a good one for your end users. After all, your website and blog is your storefront online for your clients. You want to make sure that if you get them to the front door, they can actually walk inside and look around!

CHAPTER TWENTY-TWO

Back, Back, Back It Up! (Backup Your Blog, That Is.)

Getting down to business, this one is a task without a lot of creative energy required, and yet it is absolutely essential for you and your business.

Back, back, back it up! Do you have a plan in place to backup your blog? What if your hosting company disappeared tomorrow? Or what happens if their server dies, and their backups are all 6 months old, and you lose everything? What if you go to update WordPress and BOOM! your whole blog is gone? Or a hacker gets in to your site, and deletes everything?

While the likelihood of these things happening is low, they could still happen. I've actually been through the hosting company / server disappearing situation back in 2001, and let me tell you – it suuuuuuucks.

When I ran my blog hosting company, we had people accidentally blow up their websites from time to time, and one person managed to do it just as the daily & weekly backup happened – so we had to resort to the monthly backup to restore their site. They lost 2-3 weeks worth of content. At least we recovered a lot of it, but those few weeks were never seen again. It was a little heartbreaking.

Plugins To Help You Backup Your Blog

First a little lesson about your WordPress blog – it actually has two main components to it – the Theme, which is the design, the look & feel, the plugins, the widgets, your CSS, your logo, all that stuff that impacts how it looks – and the Database, which is where your posts actually live.

Logging in to your hosting account and backing up the WordPress directory will only capture the theme elements, the design, the graphics. You need to backup the database too, and that is a little harder to do directly from your hosting company unless you have some geek fu experience.

Fortunately, wise geek fu people have created backup plugins for WordPress! Yay!!!

(Imagine me running around like Kermit, wildly flailing my arms in the air. That is how excited I am about these plugins!)

Backup Buddy: this is the one you probably hear the most about out there. It is not free, and it isn't as user-friendly as some of the other ones. That is the trade-off for the fact that it is full of great features. It will back up your entire site (the whole WordPress install, all the content, the themes, the plugins, the widgets, the database, all of it), they include storage for your backups, AND it also does a malware scan for you when backing things up. My favorite part is to do a full restoration it is just a matter of uploading backup files to your web server and then pointing your browser to the importbuddy.php file website address. Bam! Magic.

(https://ithemes.com/purchase/backu pbuddy/)

Backup Scheduler: Free, faster to configure, and full of features as well. It will back up your whole WordPress install, the database, all the good stuff that we want. The down side? There is not a built in restore tool. You would have to get your website online manually, but there are tools out there to help you do this. phpMyAdmin would help you upload your database into the Web-based interface. You can copy the remaining files/folders to the server through FTP. Plus it is free. (https://wordpress.org/plugins/backu p-scheduler/)

VaultPress: this one is from Automattic, the people that make WordPress. It involves a monthly fee, but if your blog is your business, this extra insurance is worth it! It also backs everything up, and it does it in real time. Write a blog post? It backs it up. Sign up for the premium service and it will check your site for malicious code as well as other features. If anything happens, they make it easy to get back online. (https://vaultpress.com/)

You really can't go wrong with any of them, and the best thing? You'll have peace of mind knowing that your website is safe! So back, back, back it up!

But Christine, I use Blogger or SquareSpace! How can I back it up? Yeah, sorry about that. I have no idea. I am sure that they both have their options for it though, so be sure to find out and back it up!

HOMEWORK

Choose one of these options and back up your blog. Don't put it off any longer. Do it today.

CHAPTER TWENTY-THREE

Clean Up Your Categories

You're just happily writing your latest & greatest blog post, and you decide to add yet another category to your blog for this post. After all, you're going to be talking about this ALL the time, right?

Yes! New category it is!

Noooooooooooooooooooo… Don't do it. Resist the temptation. Don't add more categories, at least not yet! Why?

Because otherwise you'll end up in the quagmire I discovered when I did this step myself. It turns out that over the years, I had added approximately 70+ categories to my blog. Many of those categories had only one or two posts in them. That meant, if I wanted to create a category list to make things easy for my site's readers to find? Oh goodness. That list was going to be a LONG one!

Clean up the categories on your blog to help make the good stuff easier for your readers to find!

How to Clean Up Your Categories On Your Blog

The first step is probably the most important – you want to check the permalink structure on your blog. If the Category is part of the URL for your individual blog posts? You're going to want to change the Permalink structure and make sure that you redirect those posts so you don't lose SEO ranking on them. (I know that possibly just sounded like a bunch of gibberish. Read what Yoast has to say on how to change your WordPress Permalink Structure here: https://yoast.com/changewordpress-permalink-structure/ and permalink structure in The Definitive Guide To Higher Rankings For WordPress Sites: http://yoast.com/articles/wordpress-seo/#permalink-structure

In other words, if your blog post address is http://ChristineTremoulet.com/category/blogpostname/ you're going to have to make some changes, because you really want all of those posts to go to http://ChristineTremoulet.com/blogpostname/ before you go moving them around in categories and breaking all the links.

Once I had that part all set up thanks to some redirects, then I could go through and move posts around. In my WordPress dashboard, I went to Posts >> Categories. I looked for every category that has only 1-2 posts listed for it. Clicking on the Posts number on the far right showed me the exact posts assigned to that category. For each post, I chose the "Quick Edit" option under the post title and selected the larger category that I wanted that post to be assigned. I had mapped out in advance my big main categories, the ones with subjects that I do talk about most often.

Then as I assigned new categories to the posts, I knew which category I wanted them in. Tedious? Yes. I still have far too many categories right now. I'm editing them down though still!

A Future Plan For Your Blog Categories

My new policy is that I keep a list of main, high level categories and all of my posts go within them. Ideally, this list should be under 20 categories. If I discover that I'm writing about a particular topic more than 5-10 times, I'll create a category for it then so it could be easy for future readers to find.

Adding a new category for those 5-10 posts is optional, I could use tags instead within WordPress if I wanted to keep the category list short.

HOMEWORK

Clean up & organize the categories you have. Make sure to do redirects as needed, or hire someone to help you with them. Don't randomly add too many categories. Lesson learned!

CHAPTER TWENTY-FOUR

Check Yourself

Have you ever had one of those moments where you have done something that you're really not proud of and everyone saw your mistake? Ugh.

I hate those moments, especially when it happens on my blog.

Check what happens when someone clicks a button on your website.

First up, a completely stupid mistake that I made. Lesson learned, that is for sure. A few hundred of my closest friends even received an email about my mistake as I tried to apologize for it. Poke around your blog. Read through the content your readers will see. Click all the buttons. Take every action that your clients might take once a month to make sure you have not overlooked anything that needs to be changed on your website. (I do this at the same time as recording my social media numbers.)

Test Your Contact Form

What happens if someone fills out a contact form? Is there an autoresponder? What does it say? Does it still apply to your business? Do you have an email list? Swell! Apply for it again. You are probably on it already, and you can't use the same email address, but here is a hint – a period in the middle of a Gmail address makes the email software think it is unique, but it actually doesn't impact your Gmail address. Mail still comes to you!

Yourname@Gmail is the same as your.name@gmail is the same as y.o.u.r.n.a.m.e@gmail – they will all land in the same inbox!

Here was my error — I had not read my own "Thank You!" email in ... well, I guess at least a year. Maybe more. It was completely outdated. Wrong graphics. Wrong branding. Wrong wording. Not what I wanted to be saying to people at all! When I discovered that this was the first impression I had been sending out when people contacted me? I was horrified!

Check Your Site On Other Browsers

Last year, I merged two websites in to one. Lots of content moved around in to new places, but when all was said and done, it was a lovely site with everything in place. Or so I thought. Turns out that everything was in its place ... if you were using Google Chrome. Using Safari? The top three graphics in my sidebar were missing. The day after

I did the launch, a friend messaged me to point it out, but I thought it was just a loading issue with the website on his end. After all, I could see them. It never occurred to me to ask him what web browser he was using. Or to check some other browsers myself.

Days later, I decided to use Safari instead of Chrome — and there they were. Three missing graphics on my sidebar.

I'm grateful that my friends are looking out for me, but I felt like the woman walking around with her skirt tucked in the back of her underwear, completely unaware. Whoops!

HOMEWORK

Check your blog in other web browsers. Try it on every browser you can get your hands on. Chrome, Safari, Firefox, Internet Explorer. Mac & PC. iPhone, Android phone, Android tablets, the Microsoft Surface, and the iPad. Make sure you know what it looks like in every web browser. If you don't have access to all the computers, ask your friends to help you out, or come post in our Business Brilliantly group and ask. People can do screen captures for you so that you can see if there are any errors.

CHAPTER TWENTY-FIVE

Help Build Trust For Your Blog By Using Social Proof

Whenever I discover a new blog or business, one of the first things I do is look for social proof about the business on their website. Are you sharing your social proof with your readers?

With the option for smart buttons on your blog, people can now see how many people have shared your post on Facebook, Twitter, Pinterest and Google+. You're surfing the web, you come to a post that seems cool, but then you notice that 37 other people have shared it — and before you know it? You're sharing it too.

Building your Know / Like / Trust factor is huge for your business, and social proof will help you get there with your current and future clients.

Did you know that there is Psychology behind why we share with others?

"People's behavior is heavily influenced by what others say and do. Whether you are a company trying to get people to talk more about your brand, or a public health organization trying to get people to spread your healthy eating message, these results provide insight into how to design more effective messages and communication strategies." – Psychological Science

Show Off Your Social Proof

There are a number of WordPress Plugins that you can use that will help show off the Social Proof on your blog posts:

Jetpack Sharing: From the team behind WordPress is this great plugin that gives your site visitors all of the social sharing options, along with keeping count of all of the previous shares. (http://jetpack.me/support/sharing/)

ShareThis: Another very popular plugin is ShareThis, which allows people to share your post to all of their social media accounts, in addition to sharing via email and so much more. Lovely options of where to place your bar of sharing icons as well.
(http://www.sharethis.com/)

Share Client Reviews On Your Blog

After each client that you work with, make a point to request from them a review of your services. Personally, I prefer to send them a pretty straightforward questionnaire.

Once they respond, look for sentences that you can use, with your client's permission, to create a review page on your blog. Try to include photos of the clients and their full names. This further helps your reader trust what they are reading because they know that a real person wrote it.

Not sure what questions to ask?

Are you building trust for your blog? What steps are you taking – or do you have in place already – to help build trust using social proof?

HOMEWORK

Check your blog for social proof. What can you add? How can you build the Know / Like / Trust factor even more?

CHAPTER TWENTY-SIX

Make Your Blog Posts Pinterest Friendly

Pinterest can be one of the MOST effective, beneficial, OMG it drives traffic part of blogging that you should be using. The key step you need to do when you blog?

Make your blog posts Pinterest friendly!

For every blog post I create I make sure that I have a graphic with the post title on it along with my URL. For a blog series, I also include the series name so that people know there are many posts about blogging on my site. These drive a TON of traffic to my blog!

Use The ALT Tag To Your Advantage

For each photo that you use for your site, you want to re-name the file before you upload it. A photo named IMG_8765.jpg should be renamed something far more in-formative, like product-name-review.jpg so that Google

Images picks up on it. (Uses dashes, not underscores as well, Google prefers them.)

As you insert the image to your blog post, think about what sentence you want to display on Pinterest. Use that for the ALT text on your post description - full, long sentences. Include your URL for the post! Pinterest converts them to links, and it will help your SEO ranking!

Now, when someone is visiting your website and they choose to Pin your photo to Pinterest, the text that you have there for the ALT text will be automatically filled in for them as the description for the Pin. The majority of users do not change it at all, and Google sees it as a valid link to your website, which helps your SEO.

Pinning Your Own Work

As soon as I hit publish on every post, I immediately Pin that graphic over on Pinterest boards as well. It is my way of alerting my followers over there to come see my latest post, no different than sharing it on Facebook or Twitter.

The bonus perk? A lot more people will see it on Pinterest than will ever see it on Facebook! (Unless I was willing to pay for advertising or boosting it. Sorry, Facebook, not paying for every post.)

If you use a Pinterest scheduling service, make sure to add your Pins there, and set them up to be shared in the future as well.

Creating Pinterest Friendly Graphics

Pinterest friendly graphics should be vertical, long and lean, so that they show up more visibly. Studies say that reds & oranges are clicked on more often. Photos with faces aren't viewed as much.

In all of that, I have to tell you … find what works best FOR YOU.

You just might break all of those "rules". I see photos with faces go viral and appear everywhere, and I've had red graphics barely get a single pin.

The essential part is that they coordinate with your branding on your blog. Make a visible statement.

Create graphic templates for your brand, so that as soon as someone pulls up Pinterest, they will know that it is yours. Stand out.

If your blog posts are photograph intensive, use BlogStomp to create collages of your work quick & easily. That way, it is easier for people to pin a whole cohesive set of images and not just one photograph at a time. They make a great impression and really stand out on Pinterest too! (http://www.christinetremoulet.com/blogstomp)

I love BlogStomp for this because it is a quick, easy to use, stand-alone app. No extra software required! Get stomping!

No matter what you use? Make sure your blog posts are Pinterest friendly. It is the best way to draw visitors to your blog!

HOMEWORK

How Pinterest friendly are your top 3 posts on your blog? Update them with Pinterest friendly graphics that match your current brand. Create Pinterest templates that are branded for your business in Canva.com or whatever graphic creating software you prefer.

CHAPTER TWENTY-SEVEN

Create A Call To Action

Yay! Someone has found your website! A new reader, happy happy joy joy! They read your latest post, and maybe – if you're lucky – they even left a comment. Great!

Uhm… now what? What do you want them to do next?

Does your site have a clear call to action?

I'm not talking yellow highlighter graphics and big red arrows. Flashing, blinking animated GIFs are out too.

Just words. Clear, plain, simple words. Guide people and tell them what you want them to do next. "Enjoy this post? Be sure to sign up for my newsletter." or maybe "Interested in booking your own session? Contact me here to set yours up today!"

There are three key things you want to do with your call to action:

(1) Tell people what to do next. Click the button below. Contact me here. Clear, concise, action.

(2)   Encourage them to do it right away. Once they leave your site? It is harder to bring them back.

(3)   Depending on your call to action, a statement that removes or reduces risk. A free trial, no obligation.

Give them a reason to stay, and they will keep coming back for more!

You should have a call to action at the end of every single post you write. It does not have to be the same thing every time, as your goal with each post may be a little different. Or it can be the same thing every time if that fits you best.

For example, I want you to sign up for my newsletter – so that is what is at the end of every post. Think about what you want them to do next – and tell them.

One more tip – if you want them to contact you? Put the link to your contact page right there in your call to action. Don't make them scroll back up to the top to find it in your navigation menu.

The easier you make it, the more likely people are to do it!

HOMEWORK

How clear are the calls to action on your home page and in each post? How can you switch them up so they are not the same each time? Do your most popular posts have a call to action on them? If not, add one today!

CHAPTER TWENTY-EIGHT

Blogging's Impact On Your Website's SEO

You may have wondered why we haven't talked at much about SEO until now. It is a decision I made quite intentionally.

SEO has changed so much in the past 5-10 years. It used to be that you could make sure you put some keywords in your blog post title, sprinkle them through your post, and viola! Google loved you.

That is no longer the case.

Now website usability is one of the more important factors in SEO; which is why I focused on that first.

Search Engine Optimization is all about the long haul these days. The factors that go in to it might just surprise you, because it is no longer just about your website and things that you can control.

SEOmoz - http://moz.com - is a website that spends all of their resources dedicated to studying SEO. They released information in 2014 based on a variety of research that they had been doing.

What is most shocking is that only 15% of what you rank for is based on things that you do on your website. 15% is based on on-page keyword use.

Only 15%.

A quick review of their information reveals that as far as SEO goes, what happens off your site matters more than what's on it.

The latest studies of what Google uses for its ranking shows that having a helpful website, one that will provide solid, valuable information to those people doing searches will help you rank much higher than anything else.

It is important to tell the world that you are an expert on your topic, and then continue to demonstrate it, often. Compelling content is absolutely critical for your website -and then making sure that other people see it, so that they can share it too.

What people say about you is more important than what you say about yourself.

One of the best resources I have ever seen on optimizing your website is here:
https://moz.com/blog/visual-guideto-keyword-targeting-onpageoptimization

12 Things You Can Do On Your Blog To Help Your SEO

These 12 tips will help you improve your ranking for your pages. One important thing to keep in mind is that Google ranks individual pages on your site, not the whole site. This gives you even more opportunities to rank for phrases important to you. Do not stuff all of your keywords in one post. Above all, write quality content for your readers, which will help you the most in your SEO benefits!

1.   Research your keywords by using the Google Keyword Planner to see what keywords are searched for by people; select one word or phrase to focus on in your post (https://adwords.google.com/KeywordPlanner)

2.   Use the keyword in your blog post title

3.   Use the keyword in the URL for the post

4.   Use the WordPress SEO plugin by Yoast to add the keyword in your meta description. While this doesn't help your SEO directly, the meta description is also what Google displays to people for their search results and if well-worded it will encourage people to click on it (https://yoast.com/wordpress/plugins /seo/)

5.   Make sure that at least one subheader uses the keyword as well

6.   Use the keyword in the copy of the post

7.   Longer posts rank better - write a minimum of 500 words; the best ranking are often 1500-2000 words in length

8.   Do not have duplicate content on your website – remove duplicate content pages and redirect them to the one page that you want Google to see

9.   Optimize your images - customize the file name with words and hyphens; use descriptive ALT text with your URL for the benefit of Pinterest

10.   Update your content - verify old posts to make sure the information is relevant and accurate; Google will take in to consideration how recently an update has been performed

11.   Create external links to authority sites - this increases the trust for your site by search engines

12.   Link within your own site: if you write fresh content about a topic you have discussed previously, link to previous posts from within the new post

HOMEWORK

Are you following all 12 of the guides above to good SEO? If not, try adding a few into your workflow. Update your popular posts with these practices to help boost them even more. Any questions? Come visit the Business Brilliantly group and we can talk about them.

CHAPTER TWENTY-NINE

Look Outside Your Industry For Inspiration

When you're building your website or your blog, do you just look at what other people in your industry are doing? What about when you're writing your blog posts? Are they the same as what everyone else is writing and saying?

I get it. When you first start to plan out your website, you look at what other successful people are doing and you try to emulate it. That is how people have been doing things for hundreds of years. Apprentices did things the same way their mentors did. Changed things up a bit, but that is where they started.

That is all well and good, but the Internet? It is a wide open frontier. You want to stand out. You want to be seen as unique. You want to be memorable!

You're not going to do that if you're doing the exact same thing everyone else is doing.

Go outside of your industry to look for inspiration and ideas. For example, as a professional photographer, I read Copyblogger regularly. I look at fashion & travel magazines. I study websites of car companies. None of them are in my industry – but inspiration can be found on all of them!

If you look at what others are doing, you can find things that you can do that will be unique to you and that will set you apart. Viola! You stand out. You get the attention you deserve!

HOMEWORK

Select a magazine or website outside of your industry and look for five topics that you could write about for your industry. Find inspiration in what others are creating.

CHAPTER THIRTY

Beyond The Blog

Congratulations! You've reached Day 30, and you're now equipped with the knowledge to start blogging brilliantly for your business success. Your blog is such a powerful tool for engaging with your audience.

Between your blog and your email list, you have an amazing platform to connect with new customers and retain old ones. Keep up the conversation via emails and blog posts, and give your clients an easy way to discover what you offer that they need most!

Are you ready to add a little more oomph to your outreach tool belt? Here are some additional things that you can do to add to your blog or as a special treat for your blog readers. After all, not all of your content has to be in written form!

Options to Consider

There are so many options to consider! Choose from them the ones that are right for you. Continue to build your Know / Like / Trust factor to connect with your clients!

YouTube Videos: turn the camera on yourself and share your expertise in videos in one of the most searched sites on the Internet. People can subscribe to your YouTube channel, and you can embed the videos on your blog.

Podcasting: Maybe you prefer to do audio recordings over videos? This format is great if you have always dreamed of having your own radio show. You can then share your Podcast through iTunes (for iPhones) and Stitcher (for Android) and other podcasting services such as SoundCloud, and embed them in your blog to deliver them to your readers.

Webinars: Have a mini course you would like to teach in an engaging format for your viewers? Webinars are a huge hit. You can then record them for display later on your website, or set them up for sale through a service like Vimeo.

Google Hangouts: Another great live option, with more interaction and engagement for your viewers.

Create a Facebook Group: Managing a Facebook group takes time to build a community, but if it is a great fit for you and your message, this can be a wonderful medium to bring like-minded individuals together. Facebook also tends to share group updates more than Page updates in the Timeline for users to view.

Write a book: You can then choose to sell it through your website or through Amazon, depending on which is the best fit for spreading your message.

Speak at a conference: There are conferences out there for every topic you can imagine. Find the ones that are the perfect fit for you and research what it takes to apply to them.

Organize an event: Bring your community together in person, or start a small intimate gathering for your ideal clients; the bonds that come out of meeting up in person run deep.

Nobody said being an industry leader would be easy, but if you enjoy creating content and creating solutions for your clients, it's well worth the work, and you can have a lot of fun along the way! Learn, evolve, succeed. You've got this!

HOMEWORK

Do any of these feel like a good fit for you and your audience? Would you enjoy learning more about the steps to succeed with the above outreach options? Share what you want to learn more about or what you are doing beyond the blog, in the Business Brilliantly Facebook group at http://Facebook.com/groups/BusinessBrilliantly

Thank you so much for joining me on this journey to improve your blog. I'm looking forward to sharing all kinds of goodness with you moving forward!

Interested in Learning More About Running Your Business Brilliantly?

The Business Brilliantly mission is built around the mindset of defining your own success and building your business around the life that you desire. Working together to find clarity in your message to the world, the beautiful difference that makes you stand out, and building your brand and marketing techniques around you, make you an unstoppable force in your industry. Anyone can do what you do, but no one can be who you are.

Christine offers regular blog posts, podcasts, books, group programs, and one-on-one coaching to help you get your business where you want to be. Learn more, read the blog, and join the newsletter to stay up to date on exclusive information, announcements, classes, and coaching opportunities at http://ChristineTremoulet.com

ABOUT THE AUTHOR

Christine Tremoulet started her personal blog in 2000, while working as a Web Consultant with Fortune 500 Companies. When she stepped out as her own boss as a professional photographer, she found that the power of blogging and sharing her stories, especially the vulnerable ones, was key to standing out in an otherwise crowded market. With work featured in publications such as the *New York Times* and the *Houston Chronicle*, a seasoned writer and speaker, Christine coaches and teaches creative entrepreneurs, especially photographers, storytelling marketing to grow their business with confidence.

Connect with her at www.ChristineTremoulet.com